Something for Everyone

by
The Devoted Cook

Dedication

I would like to dedicate this cookbook to my family
and friends who supported me in my vision
to open a cafe. The experience I gained
changed my life by connecting me to so
many amazing people that continue to bless me.
I love and appreciate all of you!

*Each one should use whatever gift he has received to serve others,
faithfully administering God's grace in its various forms.*
1 Peter 4:10-11

Table of Contents

I Get By with a Little Help from My Friends

The Road Less Traveled, Our Journey to Health

Introduction

I truly believe that God gives each one of us special gifts for the purpose of benefiting and blessing others. As a young girl, I was fortunate enough to be on the receiving end of one of the many exceptional gifts God had bestowed upon my grandmother and mother – The gift of superior home-made cooking.

Both Mom and Grandma had the distinctive ability to take simple, basic, fresh ingredients and create mouth-watering home-made dishes. Just one taste of Grandma's jams or mom's chocolate sauce for ice cream and we all knew. It was more than just good cooking; it was a unique gift for the purpose of benefiting others.

I am so grateful that my mom had me helping her in the kitchen early on. She carefully taught me how to prepare long-time family favorites such as Taglorini and Grandma's Sweet Rolls. I was very mindful to watch mom and grandma closely as they exercised their gifts in the kitchen. A dash of seasoning here, a sprinkle of sugar there, a pat of butter, a splash of cream. It was amazing.

By the time I was in my early 20's, I was quite accustomed to working in the kitchen myself and I began throwing various parties primarily centered around food.

While my love for cooking grew as I planned parties, using the home-made dishes that I learned from mom and grandma, I didn't actually realize just how passionate I was about cooking until many years later. And I certainly never considered that God may have gifted me in the area of cooking like he had with mom and grandma until I began feeling a tug on my heart to open a café & catering business.

At first, it didn't seem to make any sense to me because I was working as a realtor and had no professional experience in running a café & catering business. Besides, Mom and Grandma had the gift of blessing others with their cooking, not me. Right?

Apparently I was wrong on that assumption because I soon discovered that when God decides to gift you in an area and wants you to use it to bless others, you can either try to ignore God's persistent calling upon your heart, or you can choose to embrace it. Eventually, I chose the latter.

In 2004, I opened Main Street Café with most of the popular dishes served derived from Mom and Grandma's special recipe collection, as well as a sprinkling of recipes from my friends.

Sometime after opening the café, I began to notice continual requests from customers for the recipes of the various dishes they enjoyed.

The idea of creating a cookbook seemed like a perfect solution to preserve the traditional recipes I grew up with, while also meeting the requests of my customers and friends. Unfortunately, due to life's many demands, actually putting the cookbook together would be delayed and after almost five years of building a successful business, I sold the cafe.

Still, the dream of creating a cookbook remained in my heart. As God would have it, the delay served a purpose. During that time, I discovered that God gave me a real passion for not only cooking but healthy cooking in order to better care for the health of my family.

Wrapping my mind around how to create a cookbook that would allow me to share my family's traditional recipes along with sharing my passion for healthy cooking was a great challenge for me. After some time, I finally had an "Ah-Ha!" moment. The cookbook would be divided into four sections following my path as a cook!

And here you have it, "Something For Everyone" by The Devoted Cook.

Along with preserving cherished family recipes and sharing healthy food options, my biggest desire for this cookbook is that it will inspire people to get back to the tradition of cooking together as a family, talking and laughing, while making home-cooked meals a family affair once again.

To contact Kerry Harris
Email: devotedcook@gmail.com
or visit my website
www.thedevotedcook.com

Mom Fran &
Gram Dorothy

Recipes from Gram & Other Family Favorites

I am reminded of your sincere faith, which first lived in your grandmother Lois and in your mother Eunice and, I am persuaded, now lives in you also.
2 Timothy 1:5

Broccoli Cheese Casserole

2   pkgs of frozen chopped broccoli
1   large box of Cheez-It crackers
1   10 oz can of cream of mushroom soup
1/2 cup milk
1   tbsp mayonnaise
1   cup shredded cheddar cheese
1   egg

Directions

Cook broccoli according to package directions and then squeeze out the liquid.

Mix together the remaining ingredients (except Cheez-It crackers). Put into a greased casserole dish (I use an oblong casserole dish). Place crumbled Cheez-Its on the top of the casserole.

Cook at 350° until bubbly, approximately 30 to 40 minutes. This can be made a few hours ahead of time and refrigerated.

Homemade Macaroni & Cheese

1	16 oz package macaroni noodles
2	tbsp butter
2	tbsp flour
1/2	tsp salt
1/8	tsp pepper
2-1/2	cups milk
1-1/2	cups grated sharp cheese
1/2	cup buttered bread crumbs
1/4	tsp paprika

Directions

Cook macaroni noodles according to directions on package and drain.

In a medium saucepan on medium heat, melt butter, blend in flour and seasonings, except paprika. Add milk and cook, stirring constantly until thick. Add one cup of the cheese and stir until cheese melts. Combine macaroni with sauce and place in buttered 9 x 13 baking dish.

Top with remaining cheese and buttered bread crumbs. Sprinkle lightly with paprika and bake, uncovered in 375° oven for about 25 minutes.

Lasagna

1	tbsp oil
1	medium onion, chopped
3	cloves of garlic, chopped
2	pounds of ground beef or turkey
2	8 oz cans diced tomatoes
4	medium tomatoes, chopped
2	6 oz cans tomato paste
2	packages of dry spaghetti seasonings
1	tbsp Italian seasoning
1	tbsp sugar
1	pound fresh sliced mushrooms (or 2 cans)
1/2	tsp basil
	salt and pepper to taste
1	pound mozzarella cheese, shredded
1	pound cheddar cheese, shredded
2	boxes lasagna noodles, cooked and drained

Directions

Sauté the onion and garlic in oil and then add the meat. Once the meat is fully cooked add the spaghetti sauce packets, diced tomatoes, fresh tomatoes, tomato paste, seasonings, sugar and mushrooms. Bring to a boil and then reduce heat and simmer for 30 minutes.

Spray 9 x 13 casserole dish with a non-stick coating and layer noodles, sauce and cheese ending with the sauce and cheese on top. (Usually three layers.)

Bake at 375° for 30 minutes or until cheese is melted and slightly brown.

Barbecued Spareribs

4	lbs spareribs
2	tbsp butter
4	tbsp lemon juice
1/8	tsp cayenne pepper
3	tbsp Worcestershire Sauce
1/2	cup chopped celery or 1 tbsp celery salt
1	medium-sized onion, diced
2	tbsp vinegar
2	tbsp brown sugar (use more to taste)
1	cup catsup
1	cup water

Directions

In a large skillet, brown the spareribs, using high heat on stove top.
When brown on both sides, remove spareribs to crock pot.

In the same skillet, melt the butter, add the onions and cook until
browned. Then add the remaining ingredients. Pour over spareribs.

Crock pot time: 4 hours on high or 6 hours on low

Inside-Out Ravioli

- 1 tbsp oil
- 1 small onion, chopped
- 2 cloves garlic, minced
- 1 lb ground beef or ground turkey
- 1 8 oz can tomato sauce
- 1 25 oz jar spaghetti sauce with mushrooms
- 1 6-oz can tomato paste
- 1/2 tsp salt
-    dash pepper
- 1 pkg frozen chopped spinach
- 2 well-beaten eggs
- 1/2 cup soft bread
- 1 cup shredded sharp cheese
- 1 7 oz pkg shell macaroni-cooked

Directions

Brown meat, onion and garlic in oil on stovetop over medium-high heat. Cook spinach according to package directions, drain, reserve liquid. Add water to spinach juice to make 1 cup. Stir spinach liquid and spaghetti sauce, tomato sauce, tomato paste, salt and pepper into meat mixture. Simmer 10 minutes.

Combine spinach with beaten eggs, cheese, bread crumbs and cooked pasta. Spread on 9 x 13 baking dish. You can add more cheese before topping with the meat sauce if desired. Top with meat sauce. Bake at 350° for 30 to 45 minutes.
Let stand for 10 minutes before serving

Chicken Marsala

4	small boneless skinless chicken breast halves
1	tbsp oil
1-1/2	cups sliced mushrooms
1	bunch green onions
1	minced clove of garlic
1/3	cup dry Marsala wine
2/3	cups chicken broth
1	tbsp cornstarch
1	tbsp lemon juice
1/2	tsp salt
2	cups white rice
2	tbsp chopped fresh parsley

Directions

Cook chicken in hot oil in large skillet on medium heat until browned on both sides. Remove chicken from skillet. Add mushrooms, onions and garlic to skillet; cook and stir until mushrooms and onions are tender but not browned, then add wine.

In a mixing bowl, mix together broth, cornstarch, lemon juice and salt, and blend well. Add to skillet. Bring to boil, stirring constantly. Reduce heat to low, add browned chicken and cover. Simmer 20 minutes, or until chicken breasts are tender and no longer pink in the middle.

Cook rice as directed on package.

Serve over rice. Sprinkle with parsley.

Zucchini Cheese Specialty

3 pounds sliced zucchini, steamed
1 lb ground Beef or ground turkey
1 medium onion
2 cloves garlic
1 cup cooked rice
1 tsp salt
1 tsp crushed oregano
2 cups small curd cottage cheese
1 10 oz can of cream of mushroom soup
1 cup grated cheddar cheese (any type is fine)

Directions

Cut zucchini in ¼ inch round slices. Steam zucchini until barely tender. Drain well.

Sauté meat with onion and garlic until meat is browned. Add cooked rice & seasonings.

Place half sliced zucchini in bottom of 2 ½ quart shallow casserole dish.   Cover with beef mixture and spoon over the cottage cheese.

Add remaining zucchini then spread mushroom soup over all. Sprinkle with grated cheese.

Bake, uncovered at 350° for 35 to 40 minutes, or until bubbly hot.

Chili Relleno Casserole

2	7 oz cans whole green chiles
1/2	(approx) lb each of mild cheddar and monterey jack
4	eggs
1	small can evaporated milk
4	tbsp flour
1/2	tsp salt
1	15 oz can tomato sauce
1	24 oz jar of any salsa (mild or hot)

Directions

Spray casserole pan with non-stick cooking spray. Alternate layers of chiles and cheese. Beat eggs and add flour, milk and ½ tsp salt. Pour over chiles. Pour tomato sauce over the cheese and then sprinkle salsa over the tomato sauce.

Cover and bake at 350° for one hour, then uncover and bake for an additional 30 minutes

This recipe is very easy to make large enough to feed 25 plus people. I buy the large foil pans from Costco and make the recipe 5 times the original! It has to bake longer of course!

Meat Loaf

2	pounds ground beef
2	eggs
1	tbsp Worcestershire sauce
1	tsp poultry seasoning
	dash pepper
1	tsp salt
1	small onion, minced
1/2	can of evaporated milk
1/2	loaf of sourdough bread, cubed
1	cup of ketchup
1/4	cup brown sugar

Directions

Mix all ingredients together excluding ketchup and brown sugar. Shape into loaf and place in shallow baking dish. Add 1/4 cup of water to the bottom of the dish.

Mix brown sugar and ketchup and pour over loaf.

Bake uncovered at 350° for 45 minutes.

Stuffed Bell Peppers

1	tbsp oil (your preference)
1/4	cup chopped/minced onion
1	tsp minced garlic
1	pound ground beef or turkey
1/2	cup grated raw carrots
1	cup cooked rice
1/2	tsp poultry seasoning
4	bell peppers (any color)
	salt and pepper

Topping

1	tsp minced onion
1	8 oz can tomato sauce
1/2	cup beef or chicken broth
1	cup preferred shredded cheese

Directions

Heat oil and sauté onion and garlic, then add meat to brown. Once meat is browned, add carrots, cooked rice and seasonings. Salt and pepper to taste. Stem and core peppers and steam for 5 minutes. Put meat/rice mixture inside peppers and place in baking dish.

Brown remaining onions, add tomato sauce and broth for sauce. Pour over peppers and sprinkle shredded cheese over the top of the stuffed peppers.

Bake at 350° for 45 minutes.

Hamburger Stroganoff

1/4	cup butter
1/2	finely chopped medium onion
1	clove garlic, chopped
1	lb. ground beef or turkey
2	tbsp flour
1	tsp salt
	pepper to taste
1	lb. fresh mushrooms or 8 oz can mushrooms, sliced
1	10 oz can cream of chicken soup
1	cup sour cream
2	tbsp minced parsley
1	16 oz pkg pasta, cooked (mom always used egg noodles!)

Directions

Sauté onion and garlic in butter over medium heat, then add meat and brown. Stir in flour, salt, pepper and mushrooms. Add cream of chicken soup and mix well. Cook on medium heat for 5 minutes, then simmer uncovered 10 minutes. Stir in sour cream and cooked noodles. Sprinkle with parsley.

Crab Mornay

1	pkg (10 oz) frozen chopped spinach
3	tbsp butter
2	tbsp flour
1/2	tsp salt
	Dash cayenne
1-1/2	cup milk
1/2	cup light cream
1	cup grated Swiss cheese
1	tbsp lemon juice (+ a little more)
2	cans (6-1/2 oz.) crabmeat, drained and flaked (or 2 fresh cracked crabs)
1/4	cup package dry bread crumbs
1	tsp paprika

Directions

Cook spinach according to package directions, drain. Place in 1-1/2 quart casserole dish; set aside.

Preheat oven to 375°.

Melt butter in medium saucepan. Remove from heat. Blend in flour, salt and cayenne pepper. Gradually stir in milk and cream. Place back on stovetop at medium high setting and bring to boil, stirring constantly. Boil one minute.

Add cheese, stir until melted. Add lemon juice and crabmeat.

Pour over spinach. Sprinkle with bread crumbs and paprika. Bake uncovered for 15 minutes or until crumbs are browned.

Serve over rice or toast.

Gram's Sweet Rolls

Rolls		Filling	
1-1/4	cups lukewarm milk	1/4	cup honey
3	cups flour	6	tbsp butter
3	tbsp sugar	1-1/2	cups finely ground pecans
1	tsp salt		(walnuts can also be used)
3	tbsp softened butter	**Icing**	
1	package fast rising yeast	3	cups powdered sugar
	or 3 tsp. regular yeast	1	pint light whipping cream

Directions

Combine milk, flour, sugar, salt, 3 tablespoons butter and yeast into a bread machine. Program the machine for dough. The process will take approximately 1 hour and 40 minutes. When the dough is about 30 minutes from completion, melt 6 tablespoons butter in small saucepan. Add honey and stir well. Then add the finely ground pecans. Mix well and remove from heat. Let stand until ready to use.

Whip together frosting ingredients and set aside.

When dough is finished, place it on a well floured board. Divide the dough in half and set one half aside. Roll out dough to about ¼ inch thickness (may vary). Spread half of the nut mixture over rolled out dough and then roll up end to end. Cut rolls to about 1 inch sections. Twist sections and place on a well greased cookie sheet 3 to 4 inches apart. Place wax paper over the rolls and let them rise approximately 1 hour in a warm place with no drafts. Repeat with the other half of the dough. I use the top of the clothes dryer while it is running!

Bake in a preheated oven at 375° for approx. 15 minutes until lightly brown. (Time may vary depending on your oven). After slightly cooled, brush with icing. Enjoy!!

Peanut Brittle

2	cups sugar
1	cup corn syrup
1/4	cup water
2	cups salted peanuts
2	tsp butter
2	tsp baking soda
1	tsp vanilla

Directions

In 3 quart saucepan, combine sugar, corn syrup and water. Mix well. Using a candy thermometer, cook until 285°. Add nuts and butter, stirring constantly until 295°. Remove from heat. Add baking soda and vanilla.

Stir very well. Turn out on greased cookie sheet. Spread with spatula as thin as possible. Once brittle has cooled and hardened, break apart and store in an airtight container.

Toffee Butter Crunch

1	cup butter
2	tbsps light corn syrup
1	cup finely chopped pecans
1-1/3	cups sugar
3	tbsp water
5 or 6	Hershey bars

Directions

Melt butter in large saucepan. Add sugar, corn syrup and water. Cook over medium heat, stirring now and then to hard crack stage (300 degree, using candy thermometer). Quickly pour onto greased 9 x 13 or larger cookie sheet. I use tempered glass sheets as the cookie sheets tend to warp.

Spread out the candy from the middle in both directions. It makes more toffee and this way it isn't too thick if done in this manner. Put pieces of the chocolate bars on top of the toffee.

When the chocolate has melted spread it all over the toffee and sprinkle the ground pecans over the top. Break into pieces after it has cooled. Store in an airtight container.

Pumpkin Bars

Bars

4	eggs
1-2/3	cup sugar
1	cup oil
1	16 oz can pumpkin
2	cups flour
2	tsp baking powder
2	tsp cinnamon
1	tsp salt
1	tsp baking soda

Frosting

1	8 oz package cream cheese, softened
1/2	cup butter, softened
1	tsp vanilla
2	cups powder sugar

Directions

In a large mixing bowl beat eggs and then add sugar, oil and pumpkin. Mix until light and fluffy. Sift together flour, baking powder, cinnamon, salt and baking soda. Add to pumpkin mixture and mix thoroughly.

Pour into 9 x 13 casserole dish that has been sprayed with a non-stick coating. Bake at 350° for 25 to 30 minutes.

Frosting

In a small mixing bowl beat together cream cheese and butter and then add the vanilla. You can use a large mixer or a hand mixer. Be sure to scrape the side of the bowl. I mix at medium to high speed. Then at a low speed, add the powdered sugar. Mix well until very creamy.

Allow the bars to cool before frosting!

Double Chocolate Oatmeal Cookies

1-1/2	cups sugar
1	cup butter, softened
1	egg
1/4	cup water
1	tsp vanilla
1/3	cup cocoa
1/2	tsp salt
1-1/4	cups flour
1/2	tsp baking soda
3	cups quick-cooking oats
1	pkg semi-sweet chocolate chips

Directions

Preheat oven to 350°.

Mix sugar, butter, egg, water and vanilla. Stir in remaining ingredients. Using a teaspoon, place dough onto ungreased cookie sheet two inches apart. Bake until almost no indentation remains when touched, 10 to 12 minutes. Immediately remove from cookie sheet.

If using self-rising flour, omit baking soda and salt.

Prune Cake

3	eggs-save 2 egg whites
1	cup sugar
1/2	cup butter
1	cup pitted prunes
1/2	cup buttermilk
1	tsp baking soda
2	cups cake flour
1	tsp cinnamon
1/2	tsp ground cloves
1/2	tsp salt

Frosting

1	cup brown sugar, packed tightly
2	egg whites (reserved from cake batter)
2	tbsp water
1	tsp vanilla

Directions

Preheat oven to 350°.
Mix together 1 egg plus the yolk of 2 of the eggs (reserving the egg whites for the frosting), sugar, butter, prunes and buttermilk. Then add the baking soda, flour and seasonings. Grease and flour two 8 inch round cake pans. Pour in batter and bake for 25 minutes.

Frosting
Place all ingredients into a double boiler on the stovetop and beat with a hand mixer into well blended and fluffy. Usually takes about 5 minutes. Frost cooled cake!

Focaccia Bread

A Café Is Born

So, whether you eat or drink, or whatever you do,
do all to the glory of God.
1 Corinthians 10:31

Spinach Dip

2   packages frozen chopped spinach, thawed and drained
1   cup mayonnaise (Vegenaise can also be used)
1   package of Knorr leek soup mix
1   package of Knorrs vegetable soup mix
2   cups sour cream or Greek yogurt
2   tbsp chopped green onions
1   can water chestnuts, chopped

Directions

Place all ingredients except the chestnuts into a food processor or blender. Blend until well mixed.

Fold in the water chestnuts.

Serve with cubed bread or crackers.

Crab Dip

1	10 oz can of cream of mushroom soup
1-1/2	envelopes plain gelatin
1/4	cup COLD water
1	8 ounce package of cream cheese (room temperature)
3/4	cup mayonnaise (or Vegenaise)
1	cup finely chopped celery
1	small grated onion
3	tsp diced pimentos
2	cans of crab (can use fresh crab if desired)

Directions

Soak gelatin in COLD water. Place mushroom soup in large saucepan and heat until boiling, stirring to prevent scorching on the bottom of the pan. Add gelatin and stir until the gelatin is dissolved into the soup. Turn down stovetop to prevent soup from bubbling out of saucepan.

Add cream cheese and stir into hot soup until mixed well. Take off of stovetop and add remaining ingredients. Stir well. Pour into desired mold that has been sprayed with a non-stick coating.

Cover and place in the refrigerator until well chilled. Overnight is preferred. This dip can be served with crackers and garnished with parsley and a tomato rosette.

Broccoli Salad

Salad

4   large bunches of fresh broccoli cut into small pieces
     (add more depending on amount of people you are serving)
1-1/2   pounds of cooked and crumbled bacon
1   large bag of seeded sunflower seeds (I use unsalted)
1   cup of raisins (more or less to taste)

Dressing

1/2   cup of mayonnaise
       (Vegenaise can be used as a healthier substitute)
1/2   cup of sugar
2   tsp white vinegar
     (I have also used apple cider vinegar)

Directions

Mix broccoli, bacon, sunflower seeds and raisins in a large salad bowl. Whip dressing ingredients together and add to broccoli, etc.

The dressing soaks into the salad and you may need to add additional dressing before serving. Be careful not to dress the salad too early or the salad will become soggy.

This recipe makes a large salad for a big group and the ingredients can be easily adjusted for a smaller group.

Potato Salad

```
15   red potatoes
 2   cups Litehouse Ranch dressing
 1   bunch of green onions, chopped
 1   tsp garlic salt
 3   tsp salt
```

Directions

Wash potatoes well and cut into 4 sections.   Place the potatoes in a large stockpot and cover with water. Cook potatoes on high heat until the water comes to a boil and boil for 12-15 minutes until the potatoes are almost breaking apart.

Drain the water and cut the potatoes into smaller pieces. Place potatoes in a large mixing bowl. Add the onion, garlic salt and salt. If you like pepper, you can add pepper to the salad as well. Then add the ranch dressing and mix together. You can add more salt and garlic salt depending on taste preference.

The Litehouse brand of ranch dressing was our favorite. I am sure that any ranch dressing would do.

We love to eat this potato salad right after we make it, while it is still warm!!

This recipe could have been part of my "friends" section since it came from my friend, Robin Fahey. Robs (as I call her) told me that the original recipe came from her Aunt Alice. Thank you Aunt Alice and Robs for sharing this delicious salad!

Main Street Salad

Salad

1	avocado chopped into pieces
1	small can mandarin oranges, drained
1	cup cashews
4	cups Spring Mix or preferred lettuce

Poppy Seed Dressing

1/8	tsp dry mustard
1/4	tsp minced onion
1/3	cup sugar
1/3	cup apple cider vinegar
1	cup oil (I use olive oil but any oil will do)
1	tsp poppy seeds

Directions

I like to make this salad ahead of time. I place the avocado, oranges and cashews at the bottom of the salad bowl and place the lettuce over the top. At this point I can refrigerate the salad until just before dressing to serve.

For the dressing, mix together the mustard, onion, sugar and vinegar. Slowly add the oil while whisking. Then add the poppy seeds.

This recipe can be made to feed a large crowd! Make sure to dress just before serving as the lettuce wilts very quickly!!

The chicken salad recipe which was served on a croissant was one of the most popular sandwiches at the cafe. My friend, Teri Allen, shared the original recipe with me and I am so grateful that she did!

Chicken Salad

5	cooked boneless/skinless chicken breasts
	(5 cans of canned chicken breasts is also an option)
1-1/2	cups of mayonnaise
1-1/2	cups of chopped celery
2	cups of sliced seedless grapes
1/4	cup of chopped green onions
1-1/2	tsp granulated garlic (can use fresh if desired)
1/2	cup chopped walnuts (optional)
	salt to taste

Directions

Cover boneless, skinless chicken breasts with water and boil until chicken is fully cooked. Chop the chicken and place in a large bowl. If using canned chicken, squeeze water from can.

Stir in remaining ingredients into the bowl of chicken. I start out with a cup of mayonnaise and then add more depending on taste. For a healthier option, I use Veganaise made with grape seed oil.

Pasta Salad

1	16 oz package penne pasta
2-1/2	cups Colby and Monterey jack cheese, cubed or shredded
1-1/2	cups salami, sliced into triangles
2-1/2	cups broccoli, chopped into pieces
	dash of garlic salt
2	cups of Greek vinaigrette dressing

Directions

Cook pasta according to directions on the package. Be sure not to overcook the pasta. Once the pasta has cooked, rinse it well with cold water.

Place pasta into a large bowl and add the cheese, broccoli, salami, dash of garlic salt and the dressing. The salami triangles tend to stick together, make sure to separate them. Mix well and serve!

If you are unable to locate Greek vinaigrette dressing, a good substitute is Bernstein's Restaurant Style dressing.

Potato Soup

12	red potatoes, washed and cubed
6	cups hot water
3	tsp minced onion (fresh or dried)
3	cloves garlic, chopped
1-1/2	tsp salt
	pepper to taste
3	cups heavy cream (use milk if desired)
12	ounces Velveeta cheese
6	tbsp butter
3	tsp parsley

Directions

In a large soup pot, combine potatoes, water, onion, garlic, salt and pepper. Bring to a boil over medium heat. Reduce heat, cover and simmer for 20 to 30 minutes until potatoes are tender. Do not drain.

Mash potatoes into the liquid until nearly smooth (leave some chunks). Add remaining ingredients. Cook and stir until cheese is melted. Delicious served with focaccia bread!

Taco Soup

1	pound ground beef or turkey
1	medium onion, chopped
1	15 oz can red kidney beans, not drained
1	15 oz can string beans, not drained
1	28 oz can crushed tomatoes
1	15 oz can corn, not drained
1	15 oz can tomato sauce
1	taco seasoning packet
1	cup shredded cheddar cheese
	tortilla chips

Directions

Brown the meat and onion in large skillet until fully cooked. Drain any excess fat.

Place cooked meat in a large soup pot and add all remaining ingredients, except tortilla chips.

Simmer for 30 minutes, making sure that the cheese is melted.

Serve with tortilla chips! Sprinkle more cheese on top of soup before serving, if desired!

This recipe can be multiplied many times to feed lots of people!!

Tomato & Basil Soup

1	large onion, coarsely chopped
1	carrot, grated
1/4	cup butter
5	medium ripe tomatoes
	(about 1 1/2 lbs, peeled and quartered
1/4	cup finely chopped fresh basil leaves
	(about 1/2 cup packed whole leaves)
1	tsp salt
	pepper to taste
3/4	tsp sugar
2	cups chicken stock

Directions

In a 2 qt saucepan, sauté onion and carrot in butter until onion is soft. Stir in cooked and peeled tomatoes, basil, sugar, salt and pepper to taste. Cover and simmer 15 minutes.

Puree in a blender or food processor until smooth. Return the puree to the saucepan, add chicken stock and reheat.

As a variation, you can cook some petite cheese tortellini and add it to the soup.

Tomato Peeling Directions: Gently place whole tomatoes into a pot of boiling water, using a slotted spoon. Boiling water should cover tomatoes. Leave in boiling water for one minute or until tomato skins begin to crack. Remove tomatoes with the slotted spoon and place in a bowl of cold water. Skins should then peel easily.

Chicken Chili Verde Soup

1	tsp oil (I use coconut or any high heat oil)
1	cup onion, chopped
2-3	cloves minced garlic
4	cups chicken breasts, cooked and cubed
1	large can of green enchilada sauce
2	cups chicken broth
1	can black beans, drained and rinsed
1	can corn
1-2	tbsp fresh cilantro, chopped

Directions

In stock pot or large Dutch oven, heat oil and sauté onion and garlic . When onions are tender, add remaining ingredients to pot and bring to a boil on medium-high heat. Simmer for 40 to 45 minutes.

Serve with a side of tortilla chips. You can also add Monterey Jack cheese, if desired.

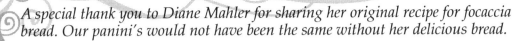

A special thank you to Diane Mahler for sharing her original recipe for focaccia bread. Our panini's would not have been the same without her delicious bread.

Focaccia Bread

8	cups of flour
2-3/4	lukewarm water
2	tbsp fast acting yeast
1-1/2	tbsp sugar
1-1/2	tbsp olive oil/plus 1 tsp
1	tbsp Italian seasoning
1	tbsp salt
2	tbsp grated parmesan cheese
1	tbsp granulated garlic

Directions

In a large electric mixing bowl (I love my Kitchen Aid®!) with the dough hook, pour the lukewarm water into the mixing bowl. Add the sugar and olive oil and stir until sugar is dissolved. Add the yeast and stir until combined. Let stand for at least five minutes, until the yeast has proofed.

In a separate bowl, combine flour, salt, Italian seasoning, parmesan cheese and garlic. Add 5 to 6 cups of the flour mixture into the yeast mixture and mix on low setting for about 30 seconds. Depending on how wet the dough looks, add remaining flour. This may take some practice! Knead on second setting of mixer for 10 minutes.

Scrape dough onto floured table, form into a ball and place into a bowl that had been well oiled with olive oil. Rub oil all over dough. Cover with plastic wrap and let rise in a warm place for 45 minutes to 1 hour or until doubled in size.

Preheat oven to 375°.

Carefully place dough onto an oiled half sheet pan and pat out dough to fit pan, it will shrink around the edges, but it will fill in while it rises. Add a bit more olive oil on top of the dough and spread evenly. Let dough sit for 20 to 40 minutes as the dough relaxes and rises to fit the pan.

Bake for 20 minutes or until golden brown in color. Remove to cooling rack immediately after baking.

This recipe could also have been in the "friends" section. Geri Van Gorkum, shared this recipe with me and it turned out to be a popular catering recipe at the cafe. Thanks so much Geri!

Strada

1/2	loaf of sour dough French bread, cubed
1	pound sausage, browned
2	cups shredded cheese (I like to use a mixture of Cheddar and Monterey Jack)
4	eggs
1/3	cup milk (I use evaporated for a richer taste)
1/8	tsp dry mustard
1	can cream of mushroom soup
1/2	cup milk

Directions

In a medium skillet, brown sausage. Place bread, browned sausage and cheese in a large bowl and mix together. Place into a casserole dish sprayed with a non-stick coating.

Mix eggs, 1/3 cup milk and dry mustard together in a mixing bowl. Pour over sausage mixture, cover and refrigerate over night.

Mix together 1 can of cream of mushroom soup and 1/2 cup of milk. Spread over the casserole dish, cover and bake at 350° for 45 minutes. Uncover and bake for 15 minutes more.

Chicken Pasta

1	medium onion chopped finely
3	cloves of garlic
2	tsp oil (coconut or grape seed)
2	roasted chickens (remove skin and bones)
2	cans or 1 lb fresh mushrooms
2	diced red bell peppers
1-1/2	cups of half & half
1-1/2	cups of heavy cream
1/2	cup of parmesan cheese (plus more to sprinkle on top)
	salt to taste
2	pounds of penne pasta (cooked)

Directions

Place oil in skillet and sauté onions, garlic and red bell peppers.
Add the mushrooms. Sauté and simmer until vegetables are cooked.
Add the half & half, heavy cream, salt, chicken and parmesan cheese.
Simmer for 10 minutes. I will sometimes add additional heavy cream
to make sure that the dish is not too dry.

Mix with cooked pasta and sprinkle additional parmesan cheese on top.

Pour into casserole dish sprayed with a non-stick coating and bake in
a preheated oven at 375° until the cheese is melted and lightly browned.

Taglorini

1	onion, diced
3	cloves of garlic
2	pounds ground beef or turkey
1-1/2	tsp chili powder
1	15 oz can creamed corn
1	4 oz jar of diced pimento
1	4 oz can sliced mushrooms (fresh can be used)
1	15 oz can of diced tomato
1	15 oz can of tomato sauce
1	4 oz can chopped black olives
2-1/2	cups shredded cheddar cheese
2	pounds penne pasta, cooked

Directions

In a large skillet, sauté onions and garlic in a small amount of high heat oil until lightly browned. Add ground meat and cook until fully cooked and no longer pink.

Add chili powder, corn, diced tomato, tomato sauce, pimento, mushrooms and olives. Simmer for 20 minutes. Then add 1 cup of shredded cheese and the cooked pasta and stir until mixed.

Place in a casserole dish sprayed with a non-stick coating and top with remaining cheese.

Bake casserole in oven preheated to 375° for 20 minutes or until cheese is melted and lightly browned.

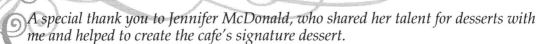

A special thank you to Jennifer McDonald, who shared her talent for desserts with me and helped to create the cafe's signature dessert.

Mini Cheesecakes

1   5 lb box of Krusteaz basic cookie mix
1   pound cream cheese, softened at room temperature
2   cups powdered sugar (may need more or less to taste)
2   tbsp vanilla
2   tbsp lemon juice (may add more or less to taste)

Directions

Prepare cookie dough as directed on box. Use a mini muffin pan to bake cookies. Place approximately 1 tablespoon of dough per cookie. Bake according to directions. Once the cookies are out of the oven, push down center with a dowel to form a cookie cup. (The dowel I use is from Pampered Chef®. Please visit my website, www.thedevotedcook.com if you would like to purchase one). Cookies need to come out of the muffin pan before they are completely cooled. Place on cooling rack. The box makes over 150 cookies and I place what I don't use in freezer bags and freeze for later use.

Mix cream cheese, vanilla and lemon juice in Kitchen Aid® mixer until smooth. Add powdered sugar, a little at a time, until blended well. Refrigerate the cream cheese mixture for at least 20 to 30 minutes in a zip lock bag.

Fill cookie cups with chilled cream cheese and garnish with sliced strawberries or canned cherry pie filling and a fresh mint leaf.

Tip: A gallon sized plastic zip bag can be used as a pastry bag to fill the cookie cups with the cheesecake filling. Simply cut a small corner off of the bottom of the bag and squeeze filling into cookie cups.

Cream cheese filling will last in the refrigerator for 7 to 10 days.

This cake is a family recipe that my mom, Fran, would make each week to serve at the cafe.

Sour Cream Chocolate Cake

CAKE

2	cups of flour
2	cups of sugar
1	cup of water
3/4	cup sour cream
1/4	cup shortening
1-1/4	tsp baking soda
1	tsp salt
1	tsp vanilla
1/2	tsp baking powder
2	eggs
4	ounces melted unsweetened chocolate

FROSTING

1/3	cup butter, softened
3	ounces melted unsweetened chocolate
3	cups powdered sugar
1/2	cup sour cream
2	tsp vanilla

Directions

Preheat oven to 350°.

Measure all ingredients into a large mixing bowl. Mix half a minute on low speed, scraping bowl constantly. Beat 3 minutes at high speed, scraping bowl occasionally. Pour into greased and floured pans.

Bake in 9 x 13 casserole dish for 40 to 45 minutes, layered cake pans for 30 to 35 minutes, and cupcakes for 20 to 25 minutes.
Cool before frosting!

Frosting

In small mixing bowl, blend butter and chocolate thoroughly.

Blend in sugar and then stir in sour cream and vanilla.
Beat until smooth and of spreading consistency.

46

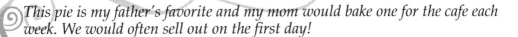

This pie is my father's favorite and my mom would bake one for the cafe each week. We would often sell out on the first day!

Lemon Meringue Pie

FILLING

4	egg yolks
1-1/2	cups sugar
1/4	cup cornstarch
1/4	cup flour
1/8	tsp salt
1-3/4	cups boiling water
2	lemons, finely grated rind
1/2 to 2/3	cups of lemon juice
2	tbsp butter

MERINGUE

4	egg whites
1/8	tsp salt
1/2	tsp vanilla
1/2	cup sugar
1	baked pie shell

Directions

Separate eggs, place egg whites into small mixing bowl. Keep them at room temperature for later use in meringue. Grate lemon rind, squeeze juice. Mix together in heavy saucepan, sugar, cornstarch, flour and salt. Stir in boiling water gradually. Cook over medium heat, stirring constantly, until thickened.

Beat egg yolks slightly and stir in a spoonful of the hot mixture. Then add yoke mixture, rind, juice and butter into the hot mixture, stirring and cooking until clear and thick. Cool slightly and then fill baked pie shell.

Meringue

Combine the 4 egg whites, 1/8 tsp salt and 1/2 tsp vanilla extract in small to medium mixing bowl. Beat on high speed until it begins to stiffen. Beat in 1/2 cup of sugar gradually beating until stiff and well blended. Spread on pie, bringing out onto inner edge of crust all around. Swirl with spatula or back of spoon. Pull up to make points. Bake at 350° for 12-15 minutes until browned or at 425° for 4 minutes.

I Get By with a Little Help from My Friends

On the first day of the week we
came together to break bread.
Act 20:7

I met Patty Dickson when my oldest daughter was just weeks old and that same daughter will be 32 on October 3rd! She has been one of my truest and dearest friends and we have had lots of laughs and adventures over the years! I was truly blessed when I answered her ad looking for a babysitter so I could be a stay at home mommy! While I wouldn't say that cooking is one of Patty's passions, she has shared a few recipes over the years that have become family favorites!

Artichoke Quiche

2	6 oz jars of marinated artichoke hearts
3	green onions, chopped fine
1	clove of garlic
4	eggs, well beaten
1	dash each, Tabasco, salt and pepper
1/2	pound sharp cheddar cheese, grated
12	soda crackers, finely crushed
1	tbsp parsley, finely chopped

Directions

In a large skillet, sauté green onions and garlic in the oil drained from the artichoke hearts.

In a medium bowl, beat eggs and then add Tabasco, salt, pepper, soda crackers, cheese, artichoke hearts (trim tough leaves) and the onions and garlic.

Pour into a 9" pie plate and sprinkle parsley on top. Bake at 350° for 35-40 minutes.

Cool slightly and serve!

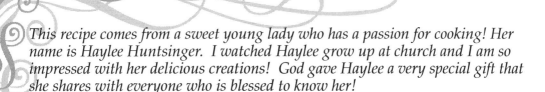

This recipe comes from a sweet young lady who has a passion for cooking! Her name is Haylee Huntsinger. I watched Haylee grow up at church and I am so impressed with her delicious creations! God gave Haylee a very special gift that she shares with everyone who is blessed to know her!

Couscous Stuffed Tomatoes

4	medium ripe tomatoes
1/2	cup couscous
1	cup chicken or vegetable stock
1/4	onion, finely diced
1	tbsp olive oil
2	tbsp lightly toasted pine nuts
1	tsp chopped basil
1	tsp chopped fresh parsley
1	tsp fresh scallion
	zest from 1 lemon and juice
	salt and pepper
1/4	cup grated Parmesan cheese
1/4	cup grated mozzarella cheese

Directions

Preheat oven to 500°.

Slice off about 1/2 inch of the stem end of the tomatoes and hollow out the inside and place in a glass dish or cookie sheet.

In a medium saucepan, over medium-high heat, sauté onion in oil. Add broth and bring to a boil. Take off of the heat, stir in couscous, cover, and let cook for 5 minutes. Fluff with a fork. Mix in lemon juice, zest, pine nuts, basil, parsley, scallion, mozzarella and salt and pepper to taste.

Roast the tomatoes in the oven for 5 to 7 minutes. Remove the tomatoes from the oven and let cool slightly. Turn the oven down to 350°.

Evenly divide the filling among the tomatoes. Sprinkle with the Parmesan cheese and bake in the oven until heated through, about 5 minutes.

In the early 80's I worked at a doctor's office with a nurse by the name of Jackie Idle. She was always sharing her favorite dishes with me and this one is one of my favorites!! I have made it for luncheons using shrimp and it is always a hit!

Spinach Casserole

2	packages frozen chopped spinach
1	8 oz package cream cheese
1	1/2 cup butter
1/2	cup minced green onions
1	cup halved cherry tomatoes
1/4	tsp lemon pepper
1/2	cup Contadina seasoned bread crumbs
	salt to taste

Directions

Cook spinach according to directions on package. Drain and add cream cheese and butter that has been cut into small pieces. Add salt, lemon pepper, onions and tomatoes. Mix well until cheese and butter are dissolved. Place mixture in a casserole dish and top with bread crumbs.

Bake at 350° for 30 minutes.

You can make this casserole a day ahead and the spinach will absorb the flavors better. You may add shrimp, crab, water chestnuts or artichoke hearts for a nice variation to this dish.

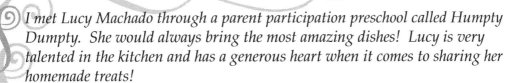

I met Lucy Machado through a parent participation preschool called Humpty Dumpty. She would always bring the most amazing dishes! Lucy is very talented in the kitchen and has a generous heart when it comes to sharing her homemade treats!

BBQ Baked Beans

1/2	pound of ground beef
1/2	pound chopped bacon
1/4	cup ketchup
1/2	tsp salt
1	tsp chili powder
1	16 oz can kidney beans
2	16 oz cans pork n' beans
1/2	onion, chopped
1/4	cup BBQ sauce
2	tbsp mustard
1/2	tsp pepper
2	tbsp molasses
1	16 oz can butter beans

Directions

In a large skillet over medium-high heat, brown onion, beef and bacon. Drain the fat. In a large bowl, add all of the ingredients including the liquid from all of the cans of beans. Stir well and place in a large baking dish. Bake at 350° covered for 1 hour. Then uncover and bake for about a half hour more.

Delicious served with rolls!

I met Cathie Davis a short time after I opened my cafe. She and her husband Gene were regulars at my cafe and I would see them at least once a week. In time, we became friends and I realized that I had a lot in common with Cathie. At the time she was involved with her church's drama group and I was involved in the drama group at my church too! Now we are attending the same church and we have been able to work together on a couple of church performances! Thank you Cathie for sharing your recipe and your faith with me!!

Just Like Stuffed Baked Potatoes

2-1/2	cups cauliflower (fresh or 1 bag frozen)
1	cup sour cream
3/4	cup grated cheese
3	finely chopped green onions
	(separate the white part from the green)
6	slices cooked, crumbled bacon
	(I've used Bacos® for vegetarians.
	Turkey bacon works really well, too)
	salt and pepper to taste

Directions

Cook cauliflower until tender but firm. Chop into pieces about the size of hash brown potatoes. Mix sour cream, half the cheese, half the bacon and the onion whites, salt and pepper. Stir into cauliflower. Place in greased baking dish and sprinkle the rest of cheese and bacon on top. Bake at 350° for 20 minutes or until heated through. Sprinkle green portion of onions on top.

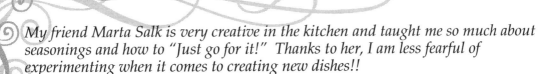

My friend Marta Salk is very creative in the kitchen and taught me so much about seasonings and how to "Just go for it!" Thanks to her, I am less fearful of experimenting when it comes to creating new dishes!!

Curry Pumpkin Soup

2	leeks, sliced into rings approx. 1/8 inch thick
3	tbsp oil
1	tsp ginger, finely chopped
3	cups water
3	tbsp Better Than Bouillon® (chicken or veggie)
2	15 ounce cans organic pumpkin
1	13 oz can coconut milk
2	tsp curry powder
2	tsp cumin
1/2	tsp dry crushed chili
1/2	tsp ginger powder (Chinese has more zing)
1/2	tsp cardamom
1	tsp cinnamon
1/2	tsp allspice
1/8	tsp cloves
1/4	cup sugar (optional)

Directions

In a large skillet, sweat leeks and ginger until translucent on medium to high heat. Add 3 cups of water and 3 tablespoons of the Better Than Bouillon. Stir until bouillon is dissolved.

Add pumpkin, sugar and all spices and then heat to a soft boil over medium-high heat, stirring often. Reduce heat and add coconut milk. Simmer for 5 to 10 minutes until the flavors have melded.

For garnish, reserve a little of the cream of the coconut milk from the top of the can and place a dollop on the top of the soup after placing a serving into the bowl. You can also add a few chopped cashews. Enjoy!

*I love it when I see the younger generation having a passion for cooking!
I see that in my friend Brook Tubbs. She loves to experiment and come up with
healthy and delicious dishes! She is an amazing cook and I love to hear her mom
bragging about the latest creations that Brook has served to her!! This soup is
absolutely yummy!!*

Butternut Squash Soup

This recipe feeds 18 - 20 people and can easily be cut in half.

16	cups peeled and cubed butternut squash
1	onion, chopped
2/3	cup butter or margarine
8 to 10	cups of chicken broth
1-1/4	tsp dried marjoram
3/4	tsp pepper
1/4	tsp cayenne pepper
5	8 ounce packages of cream cheese

Directions

Roast and peel squash. In a large saucepan sauté onions and butter until
onions are tender. Add the squash, broth, and seasonings. Bring to
a boil and cook until squash is tender.

Puree squash with the cream cheese and then return to the
saucepan and heat through-do not boil!

This soup freezes well.

*Brook also came up with a healthier version of the soup...
Cut the pieces of squash in half and roast face down in the oven with olive
oil, salt and pepper and smashed garlic. When done, puree the squash with
1 cup of apple cider, sautéed onion, one peeled and chopped
granny smith apple, 1 tsp nutmeg and a small amount of
half & half. (Omit the cream cheese).*

Janie Phelps made these recipes when she hosted our Bunko group and they were both delicious!! She sent everyone in the group an email with the recipes that she had made that evening! Thanks Janie!!

Chili Verde

Directions

Dice pork and place into large pot. Add garlic, salt and pepper. Cover and steam for 1/2 hour. Remove the pork and save the liquid.

Brown the pork with the chopped onions. Cook for about 15 minutes. Add the bell pepper, stewed tomatoes and reserved liquid. Bring to a boil on high heat and then turn to medium heat. Cook for 45 minutes uncovered. I usually cook on low until done for several hours (covered).

5	pounds pork roast, cubed
3	cloves of garlic, minced
	salt and pepper to taste
1	bell pepper, diced
1	large onion, chopped
16	ounces stewed tomatoes

Avocado Salsa Dip

1	jar Herdez (brand name) salsa verde (green)
1	jar Herdez salsa (red) (use the hotness that you prefer)
	chopped cilantro (amount depending on taste)
1	bunch green onion, chopped
3	avocados, chopped

Directions

Mix together and enjoy!!

Franco and Tedra Torrice are the busy parents of 2 young active girls. I am sure that this recipe that they have shared with me is a popular one in their busy household! Easy to make and the variations make it nice to be able to change up the flavors every once in awhile! Thank you Torrice Family for sharing this crowd pleasing recipe!

Torrice Tater Tot Casserole

1/2	a bag of 32 oz tater tots bag
2	cups of sour cream
2	cups of shredded cheddar cheese
1	10 oz can cream of mushroom soup
2	tbsp of olive oil for frying tater tots
1	can of chicken chunks-drained
2	cups of corn flakes
1	tsp pepper
1/2	stick of butter

Directions

Preheat oven to 350°. Sauté tater tots in a pan with olive oil, cook thoroughly.

In a large bowl, combine sour cream, cheese, can of soup, chicken chunks (drained) and pepper. Once tater tots are cooked, pour into the bowl with the soup mixture. Combine all ingredients completely, tater tots should break apart.

Take out casserole dish with a lid and spray with non-stick spray. Pour tater tot mixture into the casserole dish and spread evenly around the dish. Melt half stick of butter in a microwave safe dish for 30 seconds. Pour 2 cups of corn flakes evenly over tater tots mixture. Pour melted butter over the corn flakes.

Put lid on the casserole dish and bake for 20 minutes. Remove lid for the last 10 minutes of cooking to make the topping crunchy for a total of 30 minutes cooking time.

Variations and Substitutions:
Sour cream can be changed to plain yogurt for a healthier choice. Add 1/2 a sautéed yellow onion in the soup and cheese mixture. Corn Flakes can be substituted for either cracker crumbs or crunchy fried onions. Make it Mexican! Substitute cream of mushroom soup with cheddar cheese soup and add diced green chilies. Use crunched up tortilla chips for the topping.

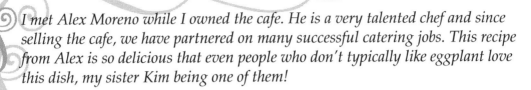

I met Alex Moreno while I owned the cafe. He is a very talented chef and since selling the cafe, we have partnered on many successful catering jobs. This recipe from Alex is so delicious that even people who don't typically like eggplant love this dish, my sister Kim being one of them!

Eggplant Parmesan

Eggplant		Marinara Sauce	
1/2	cup clove garlic, minced	1	tbsp olive oil
3	Japanese eggplants	3	cloves of garlic, chopped
1	cup flour	1/4	yellow onion, diced
4	eggs (beaten)	1	15 oz can tomato sauce
2	cups Panko bread crumbs	2	tsp dried basil
2	cups marinara sauce		salt and pepper to taste
4	oz parmesan cheese, shredded	1	tbsp fresh basil, chopped
2	oz mozzarella or provolone cheese, shredded		

Directions

Marinara Sauce
In a small sauce pot sweat onions in the olive oil. Next add garlic and cook until fragrant. Add tomato sauce, dry basil, salt and pepper. Cook on low simmer for 15 minutes, then add fresh basil and turn off heat.

Eggplant
Slice eggplant into 1/2 inch circles. Dredge in flour, eggs and then bread crumbs. Pan sear eggplant in oil until golden brown on both sides. Transfer eggplant to a heat proof casserole dish and season with salt and pepper.

Top the eggplant with marinara sauce, parmesan and mozzarella cheese. Bake at 400° until cheese is browned.

I moved to Manteca 18 years ago and my first new friend was Robin Fahey. I soon learned what an awesome cook she was and she shared many recipes with me including this delicious dish!

White Chicken Lasagna

4	cooked and cubed chicken breasts
	salt and pepper to taste
1	box lasagna noodles, cooked and drained
1/2	pound of Fontina cheese
1/2	pound Monterey Jack cheese

Cream Sauce

1/2	tsp dry mustard
1/2	tsp Italian seasoning
6	tbsp butter
6	tbsp flour
1-1/2	cups milk
1-1/2	cups half & half
1/2	cup of Parmesan cheese

Directions

In a saucepan, melt butter and then add flour stirring constantly. Keep stirring until the mixture sizzles.

Warm the milk and half & half and then add it to the butter and flour sauce. Cook until it thickens. Add seasonings and Parmesan cheese. Then add the chicken.

Spray a casserole dish with a non-stick coating and layer lasagna noodles, the chicken sauce and then some Fontina and Monterey jack cheese. Add another layer of noodles, the chicken sauce and cheese. Last layer should have the sauce and then cheese on top.

Bake casserole at 375° for 30 minutes or until the cheese is melted and starts to brown.

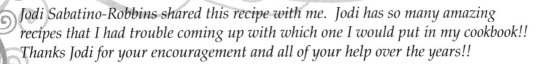

Jodi Sabatino-Robbins shared this recipe with me. Jodi has so many amazing recipes that I had trouble coming up with which one I would put in my cookbook!! Thanks Jodi for your encouragement and all of your help over the years!!

Blondie's Chili

1	large onion, chopped
3	cloves of fresh garlic, chopped
2	tbsp of olive oil
2	pounds of ground beef or turkey
1	4 oz can green chiles, chopped
1	can of stewed tomatoes, Italian style
1	6 oz can tomato paste
2	15 oz cans kidney beans with liquid
2	15 oz cans chili beans with liquid
2	cups beef stock
1	tbsp of chili powder
1	tbsp of cumin
1	tsp of salt
1/4	tsp of pepper

Directions

In a large skillet, sauté onions and garlic in olive oil until lightly browned. Add ground meat and cook until fully cooked and no longer pink.

Drain off excess fat. Place meat into a large pot and add remaining ingredients. Stir together well. Cover and cook for 45 minutes on low heat.

Also does well cooked in a crock pot on low for six to eight hours.

I have tried many banana bread recipes over the years and Robin Fahey's recipe is definitely the best one out of the bunch! This is a proven fact since we had a contest one year and her banana bread won, hands down!!

Rob's Banana Bread

1	cup sugar
1/2	cup shortening
2	eggs
3	bananas
2	cups flour
1	tsp soda
1/2	tsp salt
1	cup chopped nuts

Directions

Mix all ingredients into a mixing bowl except the nuts. Mix well and then fold in the nuts.

Pour into loaf pan and bake for 30 minutes at 350°.

If you want a healthier version of this recipe, replace shortening with 1 cup of applesauce, replace sugar with 2/3 cup coconut palm sugar* and replace flour with 2 cups of Pamela's Baking and Pancake Mix.

*This product can be found at Whole Foods or online at www.bigtreefarms.com.

This recipe is from my friend, Vicki Costa. I am so excited to share her family's recipe for Carrot Cake! Vicki is the owner of Victoria's Catered Traditions and she makes the best chocolate covered popcorn I have ever eaten in my life!! Thanks so much Vicki!!

Victoria's Carrot Cake

- 2 cups flour
- 2 cups finely grated carrots (I use 4 cups and it comes out PERFECT)
- 2 cups pure cane sugar
- 1 cup vegetable or canola oil
- 1 large can crushed pineapple - drained (reserve 1/2 cup pineapple and juice to place on the baked, cooled cake layers before frosting)
- 4 large eggs
- 3 tsp cinnamon
- 2 tsp pumpkin pie spice
- 1 tsp nutmeg
- 1 tsp ground ginger
- 2 tsp baking powder
- 1 1/2 tsp baking soda

Frosting
- 1 stick softened butter
- 8 oz cream cheese
- 1/2 box powdered sugar
- 1 teaspoon vanilla

Directions

Preheat oven to 350°

In a mixing bowl on medium, combine eggs, sugar and oil. Then add all the dry ingredients and spices until just blended. Fold in carrots and pineapple.

Cut parchment paper to fit bottom of 3 - 8 inch round pans OR 2 - 9 x 13. Grease top of the parchment paper and sides of pans. Evenly distribute the cake batter between the pans. Put the pans on a cookie sheet* and bake for 45 minutes or until a toothpick comes out clean.

*Putting cake pans on a cookie sheet distributes the heat evenly in the cake pans.
  Let cool completely.

Frosting

Using a hand mixer, beat all ingredients until well blended and light and fluffy.

Put cooled cake on cake plate and take 1/2 of remaining pineapple and spread on cake and drizzle a 'little' of the juice then spread 1/3 of the frosting on the cake. Repeat with the 2nd layer using the rest of the pineapple and a drizzle of the juice and 1/2 of remaining frosting then Place last layer on top of that and use the last of the frosting. Can decorate top with pecan halves.

***If you want to frost the entire cake, then double the frosting recipe, follow the previous directions to assemble the cake and frost the sides.
***Finely chop 1 cup pecans and put on the sides of the cake and use about 30 pecan halves to decorate the top of the cake. Refrigerate and enjoy!

This recipe comes from my good friend Lori Kelley Tubbs. She told me that this recipe is actually one that her mom, Trena Kelley, originally got from Lori. Sometime after Trena went to be with the Lord, the recipe was returned to Lori with Trina's handwritten notes. I love having recipes from my friends that carry special meaning. Thanks for sharing your recipe Lori!

Kahlúa Cake

1	chocolate cake with pudding mix
2	more eggs (besides the amount of eggs called for in the mix)
1/2	cup Kahlúa
1/4	cup oil or applesauce
15	oz sour cream
12	oz package chocolate chips

Directions

Make cake mix as directed on the box. Add the extra eggs, Kahlúa, oil (or applesauce), sour cream and chocolate chips.

Pour batter into bundt pan and bake at 350° for 40 minutes. After the cake has cooled, sprinkle with powdered sugar.

I honestly can't remember what occasion it was that I first tasted this amazing cake! Kelly Lamb brought it to something I was attending and all I know is it was the best rum cake I had ever eaten in my life!! I was grateful that she gave me the recipe!

Rum Cake

Cake		Glaze	
4	beaten eggs	1/4	cup butter
1/2	cup oil	1	cup sugar
1/2	cup water	1/4	cup rum
1/2	cup light rum	1/4	cup water
1	boxed butter cake mix		powdered sugar to
1	3 oz vanilla		sprinkle on top
	pudding packet		

Directions

Mix eggs, oil, water and rum with the butter cake mix. Place in a bundt pan that has been sprayed with a non-stick coating. Bake at 325 degrees for 50 to 60 minutes. Invert the cake and poke holes with a fork.

Combine glaze ingredients in a saucepan over medium heat and stir until the butter is melted. Let stand for five minutes and then pour glaze over cake and let cool. Sprinkle powdered sugar over the cake before serving

When my friend Vonda Van Vliet knew that my family was trying to eat healthier, she shared her mother, Marge Prins' recipe for this delicious granola! There are many variations to this recipe but I found Marge's recipe to be very simple and quite good!!

Granola

3	cups old fashioned oats
1	cup of peanut butter (or preferred nut butter)
1-1/4	cups of honey
1	tbsp vanilla
1/2	cup raw sunflower seeds
1/2	cup raw pumpkin seeds
1/2	cup chopped nuts (your choice!)
1	tbsp ground flax seed
1/4	cup wheat germ
1	cup raisins
1/2	cup shredded coconut (optional)

Directions

Spray a cookie sheet with non-stick spray, and heat oven to 350 degrees. In a small saucepan over low heat, combine peanut butter, 1 cup of the honey, and vanilla. Heat through until the 3 ingredients are melted together.

In a large bowl, mix dry ingredients except the coconut. Pour warm mixture into bowl and mix together. Then spread the mixture on the cookie sheet as evenly as possible. Sprinkle with the coconut. Drizzle the remaining 1/4 cup of honey over the top. Bake approximately 14 minutes or until brown on top. (Do not over bake or it will be too crunchy). Can be served with yogurt and fresh fruit.

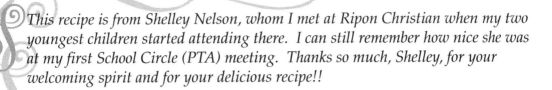

This recipe is from Shelley Nelson, whom I met at Ripon Christian when my two youngest children started attending there. I can still remember how nice she was at my first School Circle (PTA) meeting. Thanks so much, Shelley, for your welcoming spirit and for your delicious recipe!!

Chocolate Fudge Bundt Cake

1	chocolate fudge moist cake mix
3/4	cup water
4	eggs
1	cube softened butter
1	cup sour cream
1	small box instant chocolate pudding
1-2	cups chocolate chips

Directions

Preheat oven to 350°.

Spray bundt pan with Pam or cooking spray of choice.

In a large mixing bowl combine all of the ingredients.

Bake for 45-55 minutes. No icing necessary - it makes it's own in the middle. Don't test it with a toothpick! It will be very moist in the middle. Let cool in pan at least 45 minutes - 1 hour. When cool enough to remove without falling apart, flip it over onto a cake plate. Sprinkle the top with powdered sugar. Best if served slightly warm.

Variation: Mint chocolate chips in place of regular ones, and 1 tsp mint extract can be added for a mint chocolate cake.

The Road Less Traveled, Our Journey to Health

*Then God said, "I give you every seed-bearing plant on the face of
the whole earth and every tree that has fruit with
seed in it. They will be yours for food"*
Genesis 1:29

Kale Chips

1	bunch of kale, washed and de-stemmed
1/8	cup coconut oil
1/8	cup balsamic vinegar
1/4	tsp garlic powder
1/4	tsp sea salt

Directions

Preheat oven to 325°.

Line a few cookie sheets with parchment paper and set aside. Wash and de-stem kale. Cut the leaves into chip size strips.

In a large bowl, whisk the coconut oil balsamic vinegar, garlic powder and sea salt together. Add the kale leaves and toss together until the leaves are well covered.

Lay the kale onto the cookie sheets in a single layer. Drizzle the remaining dressing over the leaves.

Bake for 12-15 minutes. Be sure to watch them since they burn easily.

Remove from the oven. The leaves may seem soft at first but they harden as they cool. Store in an airtight container to reserve freshness.

Sweet Potato Wedges

5	sweet potatoes, peeled and cut into wedges
2	tbsp coconut or grape seed oil
2	tsp cumin
1	tsp sea salt

Directions

Preheat oven to 375°.

Peel and cut sweet potatoes into wedges and place in a large bowl. Add oil, cumin and salt and mix well.

Spread on a cookie sheet that has been lined with aluminum foil.

Bake for 30 minutes or until the potatoes are tender.

Mushroom Soup

2	tbsp grass fed butter
1	cup sliced onion
1/2	cup diced celery
1	cup sliced leeks
1	cup sliced carrots
1	tsp fresh thyme leaves
2	pounds sliced fresh brown or white mushrooms
6	cups chicken or vegetable broth
1	cup canned coconut milk (use the cream at the top of the can!)
	Salt and pepper to taste
1/2	cup chopped green onions

Directions

Melt the butter in a stock pot over medium heat. Add carrots, onions, leeks, and celery. Cook and stir until tender, but not browned, approximately 10 minutes. Stir in thyme and mushrooms, and continue cooking until mushrooms are soft, about 5 minutes.

Pour chicken or veggie broth into the pot, and season with salt and pepper. Cover and simmer over low heat for 20 minutes. Add the coconut milk and simmer for 5 minutes more. Ladle into bowls, and serve with green onions sprinkled on the top!

Asparagus Soup

2	bunches of asparagus
3	cups of chicken or vegetable broth
1/4	cup grass fed cow butter
1	chopped onion
2	tbsp of almond meal flour
1	tbsp of coconut flour
1/4	tsp ground coriander
1	tbsp lemon juice
2	cups coconut milk plus 6 tablespoons canned coconut milk (use the cream on the top of the can)
	Salt and pepper to taste

Directions

Wash and trim the asparagus, discarding the lower, woody part of the stem. Cut the remainder into short lengths, keeping aside a few tips to use as a garnish. Cook the tips in a minimal amount of boiling salted water for 5 minutes. Drain.

Put the asparagus in a pan with the broth, bring to a boil, cover, and simmer for about 15 minutes, until soft. Drain the asparagus and reserve the broth. Set the asparagus aside.

Melt butter in a pan. Add the onion and cook over low heat until soft, but only barely colored. Whisk in the flour until smooth, and then gradually add the reserved broth. Bring to a boil and then simmer for 2 to 3 minutes until thick. Then add asparagus, coriander, lemon juice, salt and pepper. Simmer for 10 minutes, let cool slightly, then process in a food processor or blender, small batches at a time.

Pour into a clean pan and add the milk and reserved asparagus tips and bring to a boil. Simmer 2 minutes. Enjoy!!

Paleo Clam Chowder

3	(6.5 ounce) cans minced clams
1	cup minced onion
1	cup diced celery
2	cups chopped cauliflower
1	cup diced carrots
1	tsp coconut oil
3/4	cup grass fed cow butter
1/2	cup almond meal flour
1/4	cup coconut flour
3	13 oz cans coconut milk
2	tbsp red wine vinegar
	sea salt to taste
	pepper to taste

Directions

Place coconut oil into large skillet and add the onions, celery, carrots, and cauliflower. Sauté for 3 minutes and then add the juice from the clams. Add water to cover the vegetables and cook over medium heat until tender.

While veggies are cooking, melt butter in a large pot or heavy sauce pan over medium heat. Whisk in both flours until well blended. Whisk in the coconut milk and stir constantly until thick and smooth. Stir in vegetables. Heat through, do not boil.

Stir in clams just before serving. When the clams are heated through, stir in the vinegar and season with salt and pepper.

You can use any kind of fish in this dish!

Thank you Stacey Johnston for introducing us to the Paleo Diet and sharing this yummy stew.

Brazilian Fish Stew

1/3	cup lime juice
1/3	cup olive oil
2	pounds of white fish cut into chunks
2	dozen shrimp, tails and shells removed
1	cup diced bell pepper
1	cup diced onion
1	tsp red pepper flakes
2	13 oz cans coconut milk
	salt and pepper to taste
1	15 oz can diced tomatoes
2	tbsp coconut oil
1	bunch fresh cilantro (optional)

Directions

Marinade the fish and shrimp in the lime juice and olive oil for a minimum of 20 minutes and up to 24 hours.

In a large pan, melt coconut oil over medium-high heat and add the onions. Cook for 2 to 3 minutes and then reduce heat and add the bell pepper. Add the marinated fish and shrimp and turn heat down to low. Simmer for 15 minutes. Stir in coconut milk, pepper flakes, and diced tomatoes. Heat through. Salt and pepper to taste. At this point you can add the cilantro if desired!

Enchiladas

Salsa

1	14 oz can diced tomatoes with chiles, drained
2	scallions, light green and white parts only, finely chopped
1	jalapeno, seeded, deveined and finely chopped
1/2	cup finely chopped cilantro leaves
1	lime, juiced
	dash of salt

Enchiladas

1	baked or rotisserie chicken, shredded with skin and bones discarded
2	cups part skim mozzarella cheese, grated
1	cup Greek yogurt
1/2	small onion, finely chopped
	salt and pepper to taste
6	corn tortillas

Directions

Salsa
Combine the tomatoes, scallions, jalapeno, cilantro and lime juice in a small mixing bowl. Add the dash of salt and set aside.

Enchiladas
Place the shredded chicken in a large bowl. Add half of the grated cheese, yogurt and onion, and season with salt and pepper. Mix well to combine.

Place the tortillas on a flat surface and spoon about 1/2 cup of the chicken mixture across the center of the tortilla. Roll them up to close and place the rolled tortilla seam side down in a casserole dish that has been sprayed with a non-stick coating. Once you have filled and placed all of the tortillas in the dish, pour the salsa over the top. Cover with foil and bake for approx. 35 minutes.

Uncover and sprinkle the other cup of the grated mozzarella cheese over the enchiladas and bake for 5 to 7 more minutes until the cheese is melted and the edges of the tortillas are just beginning to get crisp.

Spaghetti Sauce Over Squash

1	tbsp coconut oil
1	onion, chopped
3	cloves of garlic, minced
1	cup of basil, chopped
2	pounds of grass fed ground beef
1	cup of red wine
2	14 oz cans organic tomato sauce
3	yellow squash, cut with a julienne peeler
2	zucchini, cut with a julienne peeler
	salt and pepper to taste

Directions

Heat coconut oil in a large pot on medium heat. Add the onion and garlic and sauté until the onion has softened. Add the basil to the pot and sauté for a minute or two more.

Add beef and continue to cook until the beef is fully cooked. Then add the red wine, tomato sauce, salt and pepper and stir until all of the ingredients are evenly combined.

Bring sauce to a boil and then cover and simmer for 30 minutes.

Peel squash into "noodles" with a julienne peeler. Discard any seeds. Place peeled noodles into a large stock pot with a steamer basket and steam until the squash is slightly tender, usually about 10 minutes.

Serve squash noodles topped with sauce. Garnish with a sprig of basil.

Sweet Potato Lasagna

1	onion, chopped
1	small head of garlic, all cloves chopped
12	oz mushrooms, sliced
1	head broccoli, chopped
2	carrots, chopped
2	red bell peppers, seeded and chopped
1	tsp oregano
1	tsp basil
1	tsp rosemary
2	25 oz jars of marinara or pasta sauce
2	boxes lasagna noodles
16	oz fresh spinach leaves
2	sweet potatoes, cooked and mashed
6	Roma tomatoes, sliced thin

Directions

Preheat oven to 400°. Sauté the onion and garlic on high heat for three minutes in a wok or non-stick pan. Add the mushrooms and cook until the onions are limp and the mushrooms give up their liquid. Remove them to a large bowl with a slotted spoon. Reserve the mushroom liquid in the pan. Sauté the broccoli and carrots for five minutes and then add to the mushroom bowl. Sauté the red bell peppers until just beginning to soften. Add them to the vegetable bowl and add dry seasonings.

Cover the bottom of a 9 x 13 casserole dish with a layer of sauce. Add a layer of noodles. Cover the noodles with sauce, the noodles will cook in the oven, saving time and energy. Spread the vegetable mixture over the sauced noodles. Cover with a layer of noodles and another dressing of sauce. Add the fresh spinach and then cover the spinach with the mashed sweet potatoes. Add another layer of sauce, the final layer of noodles, and a last topping of sauce. Place the thinly sliced roma tomatoes on top. Cover with foil and bake for 45 minutes. Remove the foil and bake for 10 minutes more. Let sit for 10-15 minutes before serving.

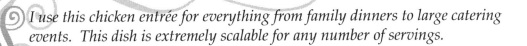

I use this chicken entrée for everything from family dinners to large catering events. This dish is extremely scalable for any number of servings.

Chicken Cacciatore

4	pounds of boneless, skinless chicken
1/2	cup coconut oil (more as needed)
1	cup flour (I use 2/3 cup almond meal flour and 1/3 coconut flour)
1	tbsp granulated garlic
2	cups thinly sliced red onions
1	cup chopped red bell peppers
2	cloves of garlic, crushed
1	16 oz. can diced tomatoes
1	8 oz. can tomato sauce
2	8 oz. cans mushrooms (Or fresh mushrooms)
1	tsp salt
1	tsp oregano

Directions

Wash chicken and pat dry. Place coconut oil in large skillet or frying pan. Coat chicken with flour mixed with granulated garlic. Cook chicken over medium heat until light brown. Remove chicken and set aside.

Add onion rings, red peppers and garlic to skillet. Sauté for 5 minutes then add mushrooms. Heat through until all vegetables are tender. Stir in remaining ingredients. Add chicken to sauce. Cover tightly; simmer for 40 minutes or until chicken is tender.

Balsamic Glazed Chicken Breast

3 tbsp oil (whatever your preference)

1 cup butter (we use grass fed cow butter)

12 (6-ounce) boneless skinless chicken breasts

1 onion, thinly sliced

4 cloves garlic, chopped

2 pints cherry tomatoes, quartered

6 tbsp balsamic vinegar

2 cups red wine

2 tsp salt

Freshly ground black pepper to taste

3 tbsp parsley, chopped for garnish

Directions

Preheat oven to 350°. Put the oil and butter into a large skillet and place over high heat. Once the butter and oil are bubbling, add the chicken breasts to the skillet 4 at a time. Sear on each side until the chicken is golden, about 1 minute per side. Remove to a large baking dish. Repeat with the remaining breasts and set aside.

Add the onion and garlic and cook, stirring occasionally, until the onions are soft, about 5 minutes. Add the tomatoes, toss to combine and then follow with the balsamic vinegar and red wine and season with salt and pepper. Bring to a boil then reduce the heat and let simmer for 10 minutes.

Pour the balsamic mixture over the chicken and place the pan in the oven for 10 minutes, or until the chicken has just cooked through. Remove from the oven, garnish with freshly chopped parsley.

Autumn Spice Bread

3-1/2	cups gluten free flour (Pamela's Baking and Pancake Mix)
2	tsp baking soda
2	tsp cinnamon
1	tsp salt
1	tsp nutmeg
1/2	tsp ginger
1/2	tsp clove
1	cup coconut palm sugar*
1	cup applesauce
2	cups canned pumpkin
4	eggs, lightly whipped
1	tsp pure vanilla extract
1/2	cup chopped nuts (I use pecans)

Directions

Preheat oven to 350°.

Prepare 2 loaf pans with non-stick coating and set aside. I have also made this recipe in a bundt pan.

Combine flour, baking soda, and spices. Cream butter with sugar and pumpkin, blend in the eggs. At low speed, add dry ingredients to egg mixture. Pour into loaf pans and sprinkle with ½ cup nuts.

Bake at 350° for 1 to 1 ½ hours

You can also add chopped nuts and chocolate chips into the batter. Make sure to use dark chocolate chips with little to no sugar!

*This product can be found at Whole Foods or online at www.bigtreefarms.com.

Crunch Bar

1/2	cup raw pumpkin seeds
1/2	cup pecans
1/2	cup shredded coconut (raw, unsweetened)
3/4	cup almond meal
1/2	cup raw sunflower seeds
1	tsp cinnamon
1	tsp pure vanilla extract
1/4	cup coconut oil
1/4	cup honey

Directions

Preheat the oven to 350°.

Grind the pumpkin seeds, pecans, and coconut in a food processor until it's a coarse flour. In a large mixing bowl, combine the pumpkin/pecan/coconut flour with the almond meal and sunflower seeds. Use your hand. This is also when you add the cinnamon.

Add in the vanilla and the coconut oil. Stir with a spatula until the mix is evenly coated. Add the honey and fold the mixture together until it is consistent throughout.

Next, add a small amount of coconut oil to your baking pan and spread with a paper towel until it's evenly greased. Put the mix in the pan and press it until it is even and spreads to all the sides.

Bake for about 15-20 minutes. Keep an eye on it though. Once it is golden brown, it's ready. Remove from the oven and use the spatula to cut it into 20 bars. Let the bars cool before you take them out of the pan.

The bars can be crumbled to use for topping for an apple crisp!!

Chocolate Muffins

1-1/2	cups of gluten free flour (Pamela's Baking and Pancake Mix)
2	large eggs, room temp.
3/4	cup boiling water
1/2	cup applesauce (homemade preferably*)
1	tbsp vanilla
1/2	cup unsweetened cocoa powder
1-1/2	tsp baking powder
3/4	tsp baking soda
1 1/4	cup coconut palm sugar**
12	pieces of dark chocolate, at least 60% cacao, chopped into pieces

Directions

Preheat oven to 350°. Mix all of the ingredients except the chocolate using a hand mixer. Fold in the chocolate. Don't worry about lumps!

Put a 1/3 cup of the mixture into a muffin pan that has been sprayed with a non-stick coating. You can also use cupcake papers.

Bake for 30 minutes. Allow to cool before removing from the muffin pan.

*See my recipe for Homemade Applesauce on page 88.

**This product can be found at Whole Foods or online at www.bigtreefarms.com.

Zucchini, Banana & Flaxseed Muffins

1-3/4	cups gluten free flour
	(Pamela's Baking and Pancake Mix)
1/2	cup ground flaxseed
1/2	cup coconut palm sugar*
2	tsp baking soda
1	tsp baking powder
1/4	tsp sea salt
1	tsp ground cinnamon
1-1/2	cups coarsely grated zucchini
1	whole ripe banana
3/4	cup almond or coconut milk
1	large egg, lightly beaten
1	tsp vanilla extract

Directions

Preheat oven to 350°. Lightly coat muffin pan with non-stick coating or use cupcake papers. In a large bowl, whisk together flour, flaxseed, coconut palm sugar, baking soda, baking powder, salt, and cinnamon. Add zucchini and banana and stir to combine. In a small bowl, whisk together milk, egg, and vanilla. Add milk mixture to flour mixture and stir until combined.

Divide batter among muffin cups. Bake until a toothpick inserted in center comes out clean, 20 to 25 minutes. Let muffins cool completely in pan on a wire rack, about 30 minutes.

This product can be found at Whole Foods or online at www.bigtreefarms.com.

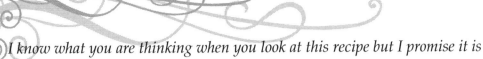

I know what you are thinking when you look at this recipe but I promise it is worth all of the ingredients!! So delicious!!

Yummy Muffins

1/2	cup grated zucchini	1/3	cup milk
1-1/2	cup gluten free flour		(coconut/almond milk)
	(Pamela's)	1/2	cup applesauce
2	tsp baking powder		(preferably homemade*)
1/2	tsp baking soda	2	tbsp lemon juice
1/2	tsp salt	2	tsp vanilla
1/2	tsp ground cinnamon	1	tsp maple flavoring
1/4	tsp ground ginger	6	oz. crushed pineapple
1/4	tsp ground cloves	1/2	cup coconut palm sugar**
1/4	tsp ground nutmeg		or honey
1/2	cup oats	1/3	cup shredded carrots
1/4	cup pecans	1/3	cup diced apple
	(or nut of your choice!)	1/4	cup raisins
1	whole egg		

Directions

Preheat oven to 350°. Combine milk, egg, applesauce, lemon juice, maple and vanilla. Then add carrots, zucchini, apple, pineapple and raisins.

Add flour, baking powder, baking soda, salt, cinnamon, ginger, cloves, and nutmeg. Stir together until moistened. Stir in nuts and oats.

Place approx. ¼ cup of mixture into a large muffin pan that has been sprayed with a cooking spray. I use coconut oil spray. Bake for 20-30 minutes or until brown on top.

See my recipe for Homemade Applesauce on page 88.

**This product can be found at Whole Foods or online at www.bigtreefarms.com.*

Healthy Pumpkin Muffins

3	egg whites, well beaten
1	cup applesauce
1	15 oz can of pumpkin
1/2	cup coconut palm sugar*
2	cups gluten free flour (Pamela's Baking and Pancake Mix)
2	tsp baking powder
2	tsp cinnamon
1	tsp baking soda
1	tsp salt
1	cup finely chopped pecans

Directions

Preheat oven to 350°.

In a large mixing bowl, beat eggs. Add pumpkin, coconut palm sugar and applesauce. Mix well.

Then add flour, baking powder, cinnamon, baking soda and salt. Mix well. Then fold in nuts.

Pour 1/2 cup into prepared muffin tins (or use cupcake papers) and bake for 30 minutes.

This product can be found at Whole Foods or online at www.bigtreefarms.com.

No Flour Apple Pie

Crust

1-1/2	cups almond meal
1	tsp ground cinnamon
3/4	tsp sea salt
1/4	cup melted coconut oil or butter

Filling

2-1/2	cups sliced apples, peeled and cored
1/2	cup pure apple juice
	dash of sea salt
1/4	cup honey or molasses (not black strap)
1	tsp ground cinnamon
1/2	tsp nutmeg

Directions

Preheat the oven to 400°.

Crust

Combine almond meal, cinnamon, and sea salt in a medium-sized bowl. Pour over melted coconut oil and mix until combined. It should be a crumbly texture. Press this into a 9" pie pan and poke all over with a fork. Place in the oven and bake for 10-12 minutes or until just golden brown. Remove and set aside while filling is made.

Filling

Place sliced apples in a saucepan with the apple juice and heat on medium-high heat for 10 minutes. Turn the temperature down to medium-low heat and add honey or molasses, sea salt, cinnamon and nutmeg. Simmer until the filling has thickened nicely. It will not be baked so be sure it is thick enough to stand up in the pie shell.

Pour the filling into the pie crust and let stand until room temperature. Serve warm or refrigerate.

Homemade Applesauce

12 to 14	apples (we prefer using Pink Lady because they are tart and sweet!)
1	cups of water
2	tsp cinnamon
1	tsp nutmeg

Directions

Wash apples really well. Quarter the apples. It is not necessary to core or peel the apples, which saves a lot of time.

Place the apples in a large stock pot and add the 1 cups of water. Cover and bring to a boil over medium-high heat. Once the water is boiling, reduce heat to simmer. Simmer for 1 hour or until the apples are very soft.

Use a slotted spoon and place apples into a Foley Food Mill® placed over a large bowl.

The applesauce will fall into the bowl. Then add the cinnamon and nutmeg. You can add or subtract cinnamon and nutmeg to taste.

If you need more information about the Foley Food Mill®, please visit my website, www.thedevotedcook.com!!

Acknowledgements

I know that I will probably forget someone, as I have so many people to thank for helping to make my dream of writing a cookbook become a reality.

First of all I would like to thank Monica Cane. Monica has been very patient with me over the last couple of years as I worked out the "how to's" of the cookbook. She also helped me with scriptures that I felt were important to show God's handiwork in all of this. Thanks Monica, for your prayers and support. I am blessed to have you as a friend.

A special thanks goes to Karen Arnpriester who I was fortunate to meet at a women's network marketing meeting. Karen is a self published fictional Christian author who put me on the fast track to becoming an author while gently guiding me through the process. You're a blessing Karen.

Thanks to my brother and sister-in-law, Rick and Melissa King, for all your support and guidance. So blessed to be a part of your family.

Thanks to my daughters Natalie and Emily for the painstaking task of typing the recipes from an unsorted collection written on envelopes, note paper and index cards.

Thank you to Jodi Sabatino Robbins for her help with formatting the recipes in preparation for the cookbook. I don't know what I would have done without you.

Many thanks to my friends that have contributed recipes for my cafe and ultimately this book. Not only have I enjoyed your delicious recipes, I appreciate each and every one of you and I am so grateful that you are in my life.

Thank you to my children Jenni, Holly, Natalie, Benjamin and Emily for your willingness to try new dishes as I experimented with various recipes while journeying to better health. I love you all so much and I am so grateful that God chose me to be your Mom!

Last but not least, thanks to my husband, Marty Harris. For some time, I told him I had an idea to do a cookbook! His gentle encouragement kept me going. He continued to encourage me even while others said that my initial healthy muffins tasted like cardboard. Marty still told me they were delicious. I say a silent prayer of thanks every day that we are together. Without him, this cookbook would have never taken form. Thank you, honey, for your love and patience.

16829489R00047

Made in the USA
Charleston, SC
12 January 2013